Dear Parent:

Buckle up! You are about to join your child on a very exciting journey. The destination? Independent reading!

Road to Reading will help you and your child get there. The program offers books at five levels, or Miles, that accompany children from their first attempts at reading to successfully reading on their own. Each Mile is paved with engaging stories and delightful artwork.

Getting Started
For children who know the alphabet and are eager to begin reading
• easy words • fun rhythms • big type • picture clues

Reading With Help
For children who recognize some words and sound out others with help
• short sentences • pattern stories • simple plotlines

Reading On Your Own
For children who are ready to read easy stories by themselves
• longer sentences • more complex plotlines • easy dialogue

First Chapter Books
For children who want to take the plunge into chapter books
• bite-size chapters • short paragraphs • full-color art

Chapter Books
For children who are comfortable reading independently
• longer chapters • occasional black-and-white illustrations

There's no need to hurry through the Miles. Road to Reading is designed without age or grade levels. Children can progress at their own speed, developing confidence and pride in their reading ability no matter what their age or grade.

So sit back and enjoy the ride—every Mile of the way!

For my parents, George and
Gwen, with love.
B.G.

Every frog a prince...
C.N.

Library of Congress Cataloging-in-Publication Data
Gordh, Bill.
Hop right on / by Bill Gordh ; illustrated by Carol Nicklaus.
  p.   cm. — (Road to reading. Mile 1)
Summary: Crocodile likes to play tricks on three unsuspecting frogs.
ISBN 0-307-26104-2 (pbk.)
[1. Crocodiles—Fiction. 2. Frogs—Fiction.] I. Nicklaus,
Carol, ill. II. Title. III. Series.
PZ7.G6485Ho   1999
[E]—dc21   98-28828
                                                         CIP
                                                         AC

A GOLDEN BOOK • New York
Golden Books Publishing Company, Inc. New York, New York 10106

ISBN: 0-307-26104-2

A MCMXCIX

Hop
Right On

by Bill Gordh
illustrated by Carol Nicklaus

Crocodile goes
down the river,
looking.

She sees three frogs,
catching flies.

Want a ride?

Okay, they say,
and hop right on.

Three frogs smiling,
ready for a ride.

Glub, glub, glub.

Down to the bottom.

Splub, splub, splub.

Up to the top.

The next day
Crocodile goes
down the river,
looking.

She sees three frogs,
catching flies.

Want a ride?

Okay, they say,
and hop right on.

Three frogs smiling,
ready for a ride.

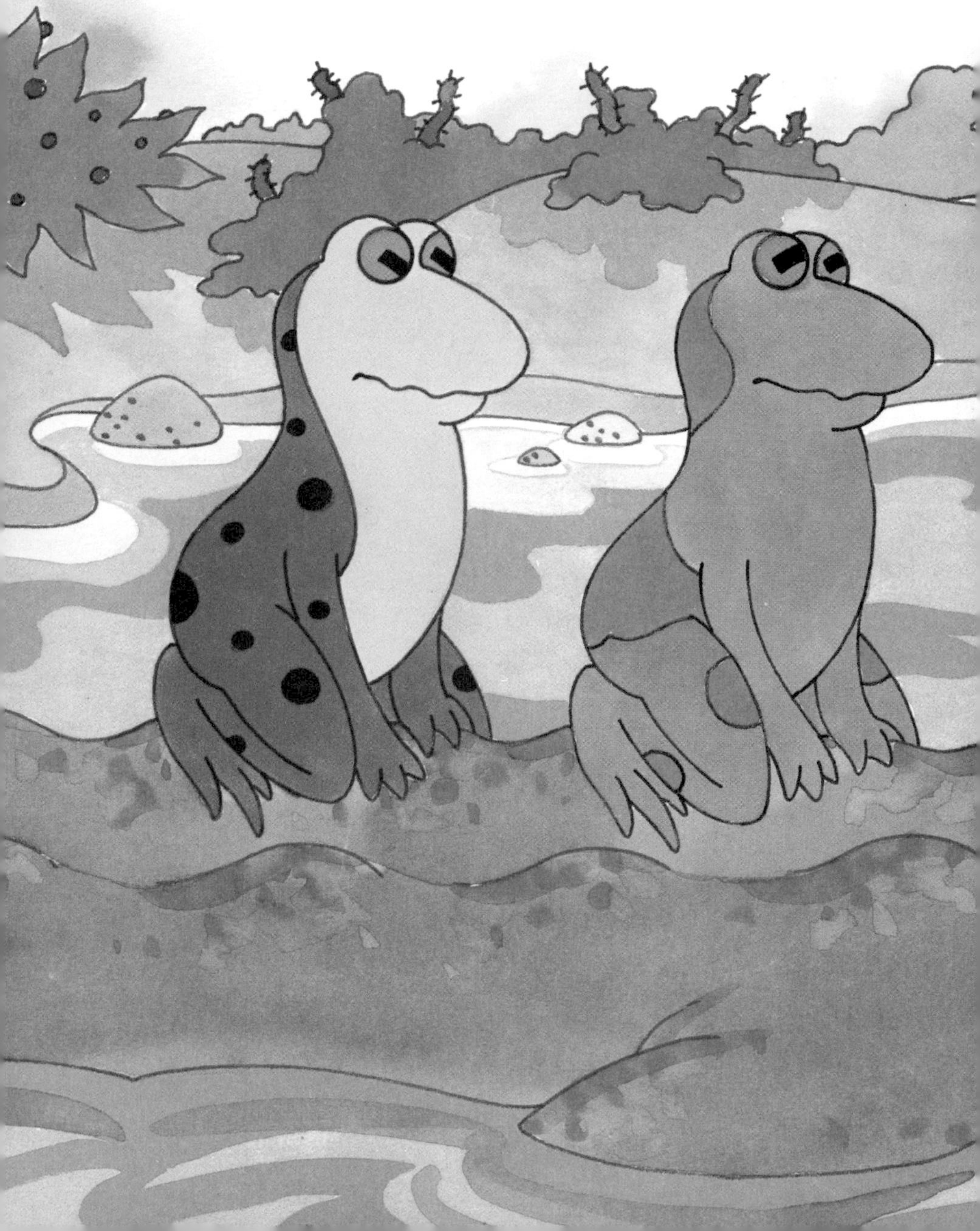

Glub, glub, glub.

Down to the bottom.

Splub, splub, splub.

Up to the top.

The next day
Crocodile goes
down the river,
looking.

Want a ride?

Do they?